ABOUT
Hartland
AND
MORWENSTOW

MICHAEL WILLIAMS

BOSSINEY BOOKS

First published in 1996
by Bossiney Book, St Teath, Bodmin, Cornwall

© 1996 Michael Williams

ISBN: 1 899383 05 0

Printed by Penwell Ltd of Callington

COVER: Tony Bawden
COVER DESIGN: Maggie Ginger
MODERN PHOTOGRAPHS: Ray Bishop
SOME OLDER PICTURES: Local Studies Library, Redruth
DRAWINGS: Felicity Young
SCHOOL PHOTOGRAPH: Margaret Perryman

BIBLIOGRAPHY

Hawker of Morwenstow by the Reverend H. Hugh Breton MA 1927
Hawker Country by Joan Rendell 1980
Hawker of Morwenstow by Piers Brendon 1975

ABOUT HAWKER AND MORWENSTOW

Of all the parsons who stride through the landscape of Cornish history Robert Stephen Hawker is the most famous and eccentric.

It is an interesting fact how now and then a character somehow personifies his or her area. Hawker and Morwenstow is such a combination. He was here for forty-one years and, in a way, he has never left. Not for nothing is this northern part of Cornwall known as 'Hawker Country.'

This is contrasting country: deep wooded coombe and towering jagged cliffs, a countryside ablaze with flowers in season; then robbed of colour; invaded by visitors from spring till late autumn and sometimes deserted in winter: the last corner of Cornwall before Welcombe and England begins.

Hereabouts you not only feel the presence of 'Passon' Hawker – as we Cornish call him – you begin to understand Cornwall is not just another English county but a people and a place apart. In the bones of the coastline and the landscape is a Celtic something – and don't be put off by what we call bad weather, for this cliffscape wears a storm well.

Beginning his priesthood at Morwenstow in 1834, Hawker came, in the words of a contributor to *John Bull*, to *'a manse in ruins and partly used as a barn; a parish peopled by wreckers and dissenting Bryanites; and a venerable church, deserted and ill-cared for amidst a heap of weeds and nettles.'* The next four decades saw a ministry punctuated by vigour and generosity as well as eccentricity. In his broadbrimmed hat, fisherman's jersey, knee-high boots and claret coloured coat with tails, Hawker became one of the best-known, most talked-about clerics in the kingdom. His exploits coping with shipwrecked sailors alone made him a legend in his lifetime.

Eagle and dove were entwined, said Sabine Baring-Gould. Hawker's gentler side was certainly reflected in his dealings with children. His storytelling held them spellbound and mothers often called the parson to help in getting the children to swallow their medicine. His dealings with Non-Conformists brought out another side. Once, for example, when questioned on the qualities of John Wesley, he retorted: 'Tell me about Wesley when you can give me his present address.'

Nigel Tangye in his excellent book *Voyage into Cornwall's Past*, published by William Kimber back in 1978, gives us this vivid profile of the great man: *'He could not bear the colour black; so he dressed at first in a brown cassock. Later he settled down to a habit of a fisherman's jersey,* with a small red cross woven into the side to mark the entry of the centurion's spear, a long blue coat like a cassock, Hessian boots, various kinds of headgear, and a pastoral staff.

'Sometimes he was followed by his favourite pig. "I congratulate you," he said to a wagonette-load of clergy who thought his get-up odd, 'on the funereal appearance of your hearse.' His tastes, though simple, were expensive. His stationery, of rich yellow parchment, with faint ruled lines, was specially made for him by De La Rue: he could write on no other; and they had to undertake not to supply the same to anybody else.

'For his tea, he wrote direct to Twinings; he smoked pure Latakia. Even when hard up he insisted on his stationery, his tea and his tobacco, and would order crimson gauntlets or a Greek Orthodox hat to be specially made for him by the best hatters and glove-makers in London.'

Hawker's name first appeared in the registers in June 1835: a baptism of William and Hester Wickett's daughter Hester.

He had come to a parish with this background of smuggling and wrecking, non-conformity and a degree of poverty. Apart from the owners of manors like Eastaway and Marsland, Stanbury and Tonacombe his people were mostly farmers and labourers – and many of the labourers were poverty stricken. Only rarely did the word 'gentleman' appear in his registers. Immediately he identified himself with the people and the place, and for the next four decades he proceeded to put Morwenstow on the map – and himself into the history books as one of the most colourful figures of all time in the Westcountry.

In his book *Footprints of Former Men*, he offered some interesting thoughts on why so many seventeenth century parsons were eccentric. These men were often a long way from civilisation and roads were rough, many of their livings almost inaccessible.

ROBERT Stephen Hawker: memories of the great man are everywhere, in and around the parish of Morwenstow – in the church and churchyard, in the countryside and on the jagged coastline. He had long hair but loathed beards and was proud of his ears which had no lobes – saying the Duke of Wellington had such ears and that the same feature could be traced in all the accurate pictures of Our Lord.

'Hence it came to pass that the Cornish clergyman, insulated within his own limited sphere, often without even the presence of a country squire – and unchecked by the influence of the fourth estate, for until the beginning of the nineteenth century, **Flindell's Weekly Miscellany** distributed from house to house from the pannier of a mule was the only reading matter – became developed about middle life into an original mind and man, sole and absolute within his parish boundary, eccentric when compared with brethren in civilised regions.'

June Lander in her well researched and well written *Eccentrics in Cornwall*, now long out of print, had this to say:

'Whether Hawker actually acknowledged himself as an eccentric I do not know, but he certainly played up to visitors when his reputation became known. He told Sir Thomas Acland, a neighbour, that the bees on the cliffs picked up pebbles for ballast in high winds, dropping them at the entrance to their hives. He talked to the birds, giving them names like Jacky and Tommy; invited his nine cats into the church, and is said to have excommunicated one of them for killing a mouse on Sunday; had a pig as a constant companion and kept a couple of deer called Robin Hood and Maid Marion. A visiting Low Church clergyman calling at the vicarage at Morwenstow was pinned to the ground by Robin's antlers, and had to be rescued by Hawker.'

'One should always be a little improbable,' said Oscar Wilde. Robert Stephen Hawker was more than a little. He had quirks and passions – strong dislikes too. As we shall see he was a considerable allrounder - a man of various talents and contradictions.

In a simple sentence he was a law unto himself.

As for Morwenstow it was – and remains – one of the most beautiful areas in all Cornwall. Here you will find lovely countryside and magnificent but sometimes terrifying coastline – both contain echoes of the past and Hawker himself is never far away.

LOOKING down on to the magnificent main door of the church, ▷
surely one of the most noble entrances in all Cornwall.

THE CHURCH

Sir John Betjeman, who lived down the coast at Trebetherick, loved and understood our Cornish churches as no man or woman before or since. To him they were the embodiment of faith in stone, and he was fond of quoting Comper's definition of church architecture: '. . . it should bring you to your knees at first sight . . .'

Though it stands in a wild and often windswept landscape Morwenstow Church has peace and serenity: a perfect place for prayer or quiet meditation. When that fine travel writer Arthur Mee came in the 1930s he wrote in his notebook: 'Everywhere the church is rich and beautiful with light to see and space to move about in.'

Hawker, like the Normans long before him, felt the power of the place – and left his mark upon it. Sir John Betjeman, visiting Morwenstow, felt

TWO PATHS meeting in Morwenstow Churchyard. Many believe it is one of the most beautiful church settings in Cornwall and Devon. Here you begin to understand why Hawker loved his way of life. Here and inside the church too you feel the spirit of the man.

Hawker's 'strong Celtic, catholic and compassionate personality pervades this remote parish and particularly its church and glebe.'

The church is dedicated to St Morwenna. Hawker perpetuated the legend – some say he invented it! – that the Saint was the daughter of Breachan, a Celtic King who lived in the ninth century. Moreover the parson claimed that he had seen the ghost of Saint Morwenna. As for the name Morwenstow, according to Piers Brendon, Hawker's admirable biographer, it is a marriage of 'Celtic "Morwen" (possibly meaning "white or fair as the sea" or perhaps derived from St Morwenna) and the Saxon "stow" (church).'

It is said Saint Morwenna died in her brother Nectan's arms gazing across the Severn to her native Wales. She was wise, holy and learned and her well, repaired by Hawker, is halfway down a nearby cliff. Some researchers believe this now inaccessible part of Vicarage Cliff is the location where Saint Morwenna first settled.

Robert Stephen Hawker, who preached a fine sermon, loved his church dearly, and many of us believe his spirit still lives on inside these walls. He was capable of giving significance to the smallest detail, of almost turning the prosaic into poetry. He maintained the zigzags, situated near the font, were 'the ripple of the lake of Gennesaret, the spirits breathing upon the waters of baptism.'

Joan Rendell in her *Hawker Country* has made an interesting point about the church: '. . . *if one stands square on the step leading into the belfry tower and then looks towards the east end of the church there is a distinct impression that the church is one sided.' Again Hawker had a theory: 'As Christ upon the Cross, His head inclined, so His sanctuary is built with an inclination to one side.'*

HAWKER'S VICARAGE

North Cornwall has a capacity to surprise. The stranger, with no previous knowledge, will encounter a big surprise here at Morwenstow.

Mr. John Betjeman, as he then was, visiting the parish in the 1930s, wrote in his research notes: *'Out of the trees rise the vicarage chimney stacks in the form of miniature church towers, part of the Gothic fancy of the builder, the Rev R.S. Hawker, its poetic and Tractarian vicar . . .'*

Meeting the building for the first time is a memory that does not fade – like encountering something that might have come to life out of a vivid novel by Dame Iris Murdoch. This, his vicarage, was Hawker's greatest material achievement. He built it in 1837 with his own money and, as a result, was a poor man for the rest of his life.

The Reverend Hugh Breton, MA, Vicar of Morwenstow, in his booklet *Hawker of Morwenstow* published in 1927, price one shilling, postage two pence, had this to say:

'When he came to Morwenstow, the parish had not known a resident vicar for more than a century. The old Vicarage, which stood above the Church, was used partly as a barn, and was in a state of almost utter ruin – so bad that repair and restoration were impossible.

'So he decided to build the new Vicarage on another site, and he chose the present one, because he said he always noticed that it was where the sheep and lambs lay down, suggesting that it must be a place of shelter. In many ways the site has proved a wise choice, for the water supply comes into the house by natural fall from St John the Baptist's Well in the garden, and the drainage leaves the house by natural fall into the valley below.

'The boards he used for flooring are thick pitch-pine of unusual width, the likes of which are not seen in these days; the doors are finely made and studded with great nails. He built the house regardless of expense, but he found out afterwards what was the cost of doing work so well. Over the front door he placed the inscription:

The Door of the Vicarage. On the slate tablet above it, Hawker wrote:
A House, A glebe, a Pound a Day,
A Pleasant Place to Watch and Pray.
Be true to Church – Be kind to poor,
O Minister, for ever more.

11

A house, a glebe, a pound a day;
A pleasant place to watch and pray;
Be true to Church, be kind to poor,
O minister! for evermore.

'Five of the chimneys are models of Towers of Parish Churches where he had lived before, and the kitchen chimney represents his Mother's tomb. Outside the back door he paved the walk with two large mill-stones.'

HAWKER's Vicarage. Mrs Jill Wellby, who has lived at the Vicarage since 1986, says: 'Hawker may have been a restless character in his lifetime at Morwenstow, but his Vicarage retains a beautiful peace. I feel it very strongly on any homecoming journey; in fact I begin to feel it as I pass the Bush Inn. Personally we have no evidence of any hauntings here, but curiously though we never smoke we do occasionally smell tobacco smoke in the bathroom which may well have been Hawker's dressing room at one time. Then two guests had a strange experience in August 1994 when they were awoken by someone throwing stones against their bedroom window ... and the date this happened was just one day after the anniversary of Hawker's death.'

The Vicarage, it must be stressed, is a private residence and not open to the public, but when the Ghost Club Society visited the area, Jill Wellby, by prior arrangement, kindly allowed our party to visit her home. It is a truly beautiful place and as we moved from room to room with our hostess we all felt the wonderfully peaceful atmosphere. Robert Stephen Hawker would be happy to know his old home is in such sensitive caring hands.

RECTORY FARM

Rectory Farm is a delightful thirteenth century farmhouse on the southern side of the tiny green outside Hawker's Church. This is a mixed working farm of some 130 acres which has been farmed by the same family for more than four decades. First mentioned in a document dated 1296, Rectory was then attached to the monks of the Order of St John of Bridgwater, Somerset.

Parson Hawker would have approved of the splendid homemade food on the menu of the Rectory Tea Rooms as it is now known. Since 1989 the tea rooms have been run by Jill Savage, who hails from Hartland, and who has developed a thriving business which has become a popular eating place for

JILL Savage in her kitchen at Rectory Farm. Jill's cooking skills draw locals and visitors to her Dining Room – sure signs of quality and good value.

JILL Savage at Rectory Farm.

visitors. Jill, wife of local farmer Richard Savage, provides food here from Easter until October – coffee, lunches and cream teas – and she offers more sophisticated menus for evening meals on Friday and Saturday and other selected evenings. All these evening meals are prepared to order using local produce whenever possible.

The former main hall of Rectory is now the dining area, and it evokes a strong sense of the past: heavy oak beams, taken from wrecked ships, old flagstone floors and large open fireplaces.

Jill Savage takes special pride in the fact that Rectory was invited to become a founder member of the Guild of Tea Shops when it was formed by the British Tea Council. The Guild is made up of hand-picked tea shops which meet the Tea Council's high standards of quality tea making and service. For all these good reasons then Rectory Farm is well worth a visit.

◁ *PART of the dining room at Rectory Farm.*

15

THE BUSH INN

The inn, like the church, has become an integral part of our history and landscape.

Dr Samuel Johnson probably spoke for many folk when he offered this thought: 'There is nothing which has yet been contrived by man by which so much happiness is produced as by a good tavern or inn.'

Outside and beyond the sheer pleasure, there is the social history of inns. What better way to meet people who enjoy chatting about news ancient and modern?

The Bush Inn at Morwenstow used to boast a fine old thatched roof but in November 1968 a fire destroyed the lovely roof and roughly half this ancient inn. Incredibly today it still generates an old-world atmosphere and charm.

Hawker, with his deep interest in all matters paranormal, would be intrigued to learn The Bush is one of the most haunted inns in the region.

A dark shadowy figure moving away from the blazing building in 1968; footsteps, defying human explanation, both on the staircase and upstairs; ghostly knocking on a door which is no longer there; a Naval chaplain feeling 'menaced' in his four-poster bed at night; an American visitor encountering an elderly seafaring man, dressed in old-fashioned clothes, who, when challenged, simply turned and disappeared through a solid wall.

These are only some of the strange happenings at The Bush. How the great man would have relished investigating such matters.

When members of the Ghost Club Society paid a visit to North Cornwall in May 1994 we met Jim Gregory, who had been landlord here for many years, and he told us of various paranormal encounters in and around the inn. He and others have heard invisible footsteps, very distinct in sound, on the staircase, walking at odd levels. Is it someone from the past leaving the building? Could they be part of a supernatural tape recording?

Oddly enough nobody has suggested Hawker himself haunts the inn, but we can be sure if he were alive today the vicar would make a special point of visiting The Bush at five in the morning or five in the late afternoon – these being the haunting hours and BBC Radio Cornwall, visiting the inn in 1986, as part of its 'Ghost Hunt' series picked up sounds on tape which defied all logical explanation. Moreover there was a dramatic drop in the temperature in the upstairs room where these eerie sounds were recorded.

Robert Stephen Hawker may not haunt the inn but some people are quite convinced his phantom returns to his old parish. One such character was

Constance Drummond of Stratton who recalled: 'One evening a friend and I were walking back from Morwenstow with my retriever dog. We both heard footsteps behind us. There was a corner, and we both paused. I said: "Oh, let's wait for whoever it is to pass." We stopped and noticed that my dog had flattened himself into the hedge. The footsteps came on round the corner, passed us, and went on. No-one to be seen. At a cottage higher up, I asked a woman if the lane was haunted. "Oh yes," she said brightly, "Parson Hawker often comes up after being at the church . . ."'

THE LATE Jim Gregory, on the left, talks to Michael Williams in the bar of the Bush Inn in 1986 when they took part in a radio series entitled 'Ghost Hunt'. Among Jim's strange experiences was the curious case of a particular door. Morning after morning he found it open. In an attempt to solve the mystery Jim put some wire around the catch – thinking it might be the cat using its paw to pull the catch down – but the door continued to be opened next morning. So he used stronger wire. It still didn't work. He then put three turns of thick wire around the catch. The door was still open next morning – 'and the piece of wire was off'. The next night he used pliers, and twisting the wires round and round, said to himself 'Now nothing will get it ...' But the next morning 'the damn wire was untwisted and the door open'.

RONALD DUNCAN

Though RS Hawker was the most celebrated creative character in this area, we must not forget another - or the fact that Morwenstow and District have triggered a good deal in words and paint.

Ronald Duncan, who lived and farmed at Welcombe, was a brilliant wordsmith, and a literary allrounder: poet and playwright, short story writer, essayist and for a while London film critic. He once described himself as 'an animated inkblot', and Ezra Pound called him 'the lone wolf of English letters.' We only met a few times but he made a tremendous impact and he was a valued contributor to Bossiney publishing in our early days. Above all, he was an autobiographer in the top flight. His *All Men Are Islands* prompted Colin Wilson to write 'Far and away the liveliest autobiography written by anyone of his generation ...' and a critic for *The Times* reflected 'If Mr Duncan's title is true, then his is a treasure island. As an autobiographer he was born with a silver spoon in his mouth.'

Our first meeting was for an interview feature in the *Cornish Review*. After conversation over coffee, we walked out to his writer's hut on the cliffs and he told me '. . . the storms and gales we get along this coast make comments with which I agree.'

I never come to the Morwenstow area without thinking of him - or Hawker.

In and around Morwenstow today you will find quite a number of equines - something which would have pleased the Parson - and Ronald Duncan understood the importance of the animals when he wrote this tribute which is read at the Horse of the Year Show on the last night.

The Horse
Where in this wide world can
man find nobility without pride,
friendship without envy or beauty
without vanity? Here, where
grace is laced with muscle, and
strength by gentleness confined.

*He serves without servility; he has
fought without enmity. There is
nothing so powerful, nothing less
violent, there is nothing so quick,
nothing more patient.*

*England's past has been borne on
his back. All our history is his
industry; we are his heirs, he
our inheritance.*

*RONALD Duncan, who farmed
and wrote on the North Cornwall-
Devon border, was a real literary
allrounder. He had an expert's
nose for exposing the pretentious
and the bogus and, as a writer, he
never belonged to any school or
movement. He simply followed a
highly individual path. Ronald
Duncan first came to the area as a
four-year-old on holiday. He once
reflected '... I can often see a
motionless buzzard hovering over
the great cliffs as I watch the gulls
returning from the ploughland,
scissoring the air out to sea.'*

GOOSEHAM BARTON STABLES

M any of us believe the supreme way of seeing a place is from the sad-
dle, and here visitors and locals are fortunate to have the Gooseham
Barton Stables. Gooseham is a delightful hamlet about a mile from Shop.

The stables, under the management of Debbie Hamilton, are licensed
and approved by the British Horse Society. About 35 horses and ponies are
kept on the farm; most of them are used for riding, the others being main-
ly brood mares, young stock and a few 'old faithfuls' enjoying retirement.
The horses and ponies are well looked after – they range in size from
approximately 10hh to 16.3hh and mounts are carefully allocated to suit
weight and riding ability.

Gooseham Barton is a fifty acre farm. The Barton is believed to have
accquired its name from being the first settlement in the parish and the
farm house is reputedly the old rectory owned by Sir William de
Gosseham in the 1300s.

HANDWRITING

These examples of Robert Stephen Hawker's handwriting tell us a good deal about the man. As Sigmund Freud once said 'There is no doubt that men also express their character through their handwriting.' The employment of exclamation marks indicates enthusiasm and imagination, and overall the impression is one of strength and willpower: no hint of repression. Furthermore his connected handwriting signifies a social person who likes to talk and meet others.

These two pages of his writing relate to his famous ballad *The Song of the Western Men* and were made available by the Local Studies Library at Redruth.

Would Hawker have become a greater writer had he lived in a more populated place like say Exeter or Bristol, where he would have had greater social contact with other writers and creative characters?

Would he have made a greater contribution to the Church of England and climbed the ladder to higher rank?

Sabine Baring-Gould reflected on the possibility – and possibilities. *'Restricted to so narrow and isolated a sphere of action, his powers to some extent were perhaps wasted. With more scope he might have done greater things. As it was, his originality, independence of mind and eccentricities were contained and it is difficult to picture him living anywhere but at Morwenstow in that lonely valley by the cliffs within sound of the sea.'*

How would he have fitted into the present day scene? It would be a safe bet to say the media would have offered him a platform. It's equally safe to assume that he would have been involved in major animal welfare issues like the campaign to stop the live export of food animals to Europe.

He would be intrigued by the fact that the supernatural and allied subjects command such a following today, and would understand the growing appetite in many people for psychic experience and a genuine desire for self-development. Hawker would be pleased too to see the sustained interest in King Arthur.

And what of his beloved Morwenstow?

He would be heartened to see so much of its beauty remains.

The Song of the Western Men.

I

A good Sword and a trusty Hand!
  A merry Heart and true!.
King James his men shall understand
  What Cornish Lads can do!

II

And have they fix'd the where and when?
  And shall Trelawny die?
Here's Twenty Thous-and Cornish men
  Will know the reason why!

III

Out spake their Captain brave and bold,—
  A merry Wight was he,—
If London Tower were Michael's Hold
  We'll set Trelawny free!

  And have &c

IV

We'll cross the Tamar, Land to Land!
  The Severn is no stay:
All side by side, and hand to hand,—
  And who shall bid us Nay?

  And have &c

23

V

And when we come to London Wall,
  A pleasant Sight to view, -
Come forth! Come forth! ye Cowards all!
Here's Men as good as you!

VI

And have &

Trelawny He's in Keep and Hold,
  Trelawny He may die:
But here's Twenty Thousand Bold
  Will Know the reason why! R.J.H.

Note

With the exception of the refrain (Here's &
this Ballad was written by me, under Sir
Bevil's Oak, in Stowe Wood, in Novr 1824. It
was soon after inserted in a Plymouth Paper
without my Signature. It fell into the hands
of Mr Davies Gilbert, who sent a Copy to the
Gentleman's Magazine, under the impression
that he had stumbled on the original Song.
It is also a matter of pride to me, that it
received the Praise of Sir W Scott, as "a spirited
Ballad of the Seventeenth Century." Many
other Critics, and among them† the Percy
Society, and Charles Dickens, have recorded
their mistaken but complimentary persuasion
that it was the antique offspring of the Stuart age
        † Macaulay   R.J.H.

HAWKER AND TRELAWNY

For a worthwhile modern assessment of Hawker let us leave Morwenstow for a short while and travel to Bodmin.

Here the Rev Brian Coombes, our Grand Bard and great champion of Cornish causes, offers these perceptive thoughts:

'Hawker was a poet, priest, a writer, a leader of his local community. We have had others in Cornwall. Bishop Trelawny was a senior churchman and man of national affairs; a symbol of liberty and lawfulness – again we have had others. These two are remembered, perhaps more than most, because they are together associated with Hawker's *Song of the Western Men*, we never know it as that – to us it is Trelawny.

'Here is a song that catches the mood of Cornwall, its emotions of defiant questioning and of togetherness. The stirring music adds to its force, but the words do express something real. Hear it sung by a Cornish choir, or hopefully, at Twickenham!

'Hawker may have written greater poetry; in his isolation he may not have appreciated the "Methodism and Mining" strand in Cornish life; but he was himself, that is enough. He had feeling for nature, for the spiritual world and for fellow-men; awareness of the past in the present; a certain nonconformity – "cussedness" even – he was "one of we" all right. He still expresses what we all feel but have to leave to a poet to say.

'The cry "One and All" is ours; it went up for John Trelawny, Bishop Jonathan's grandfather when has was imprisoned by Cromwell's Parliament. Hawker wrote his words about the Bishop's struggle against James 11. The truth remains; freedom has to be defended in all directions.

'Macaulay wrote in his *History of England*, "*the people of Cornwall . . . among whom there was a stronger provincial feeling than any other part of the realm . . . were greatly moved by the danger to Trelawny . . . whom they reverenced less as a prince of the church than as head of an honourable house . . .*"

'Trelawny puts that into poetry. He who does not share the insights of Macaulay and of Hawker misses the truth about Cornwall.'

*THE LAST photograph of Robert Stephen Hawker taken before his depar-
ture to Plymouth where he is buried – and his controversial death. His
biographer Sabine Baring-Gould wrote '... I cannot decide. The testimony
is conflicting. I hesitate to believe that it was his intention to leave the
Church of England before he died. He was swayed this way or that by
those with whom he found himself. He was vehement in one direction one
day, as impetuous in another direction on the day following.'*

HAWKER
THE ALL-ROUNDER

If Hawker were alive today he would be a leading figure in the animal welfare movement. He loved animals and birds. Local birds became so tame that they fluttered around him to be fed, and in the course of writing one letter he referred to a pair of mice playing on his desk as he was putting pen to paper. At one point he had as many as nine cats – and kept pet deer. Some of the cats came to church with him, and it was not unusual to find a cat in the pulpit.

He lived, of course, in days before the motor car and travelled by horse, either riding or driving. He had two horses called Brychan and Gladys, named after the mother and father of St Morwenna. Until his last years he invariably rode to Welcombe which he looked after as well as Morwenstow for a quarter of a century – right up until just before his death. In his last declining years he drove a pair of ponies. He had, for some years, a faithful dog Berg, and whenever he went to the church Berg went with him carrying the church key in his mouth which he delivered into the parson's hand at the church door. Usually several cats accompanied him into the chancel. At one time, too, he kept a pig called Gyp who travelled miles with him. As jackdaws nested in the strangely beautiful chimneys of Morwenstow vicarage, fires were forbidden in certain rooms for fear of dislodging the birds. Hawker was also concerned when a neighbour shot one or two rooks which had been reared in the churchyard. On the following Sunday, the neighbour, seated in the front pew, received the dressing down of his life. Hawker's text, that Sunday, was 'Are not two sparrows sold for a farthing? And one of them shall not fall to the ground without your Father.' No more rooks were shot.

But of all the animals in his life his special favourite was Carrow his pony. According to local legend he lavished more care on Carrow than his wife! That is almost certainly an injustice, but he loved the animal dearly. Carrow resided in a stable at the vicarage and, on duty, was either ridden by his master or harnessed to a little vehicle. They must have travelled hundreds of miles together on their journeys around this border territory.

On one dramatic occasion they were travelling from Welcombe back to Morwenstow and Hawker recalled: 'As I entered the Gulph between the Vallies today, a Storm leaped from the Sea, and rushed at me roaring – I recognised a Demon and put Carrow into a gallop and so escaped.'

Hawker, throughout his life, was very preoccuped with the mystical and the supernatural. Like many young men, he had hoaxed on the subject; pretending to be a mermaid, he hoodwinked people at Bude. For several nights the mermaid appeared, flashing her mirror and singing strange songs, and the number of inquisitive people multiplied. Hawker, however, tired of sitting in the cold night air, clad only in seaweed – the mermaid never appeared again.

Later in his ministry, though, he claimed genuine supernatural experience to the extent of seeing Saint Morwenna and, over the years, he became convinced in the power of the Evil Eye, once attributing the loss of nine suckling-pigs to a witch's curse. 'The sow which, like Medea, had taken a hatred to her own offspring, spurning them away from her milk . . . the evil eye of old Cherry (the witch) had turned the mother's heart to stone, and she let them die one by one . . .'

Healing and charming, dowsing and ley lines, all these are fashionable subjects in North Cornwall today. We can guess that mysticism and allied occult subjects dominated in Hawker's day too. Not surprising then that the great man should have written a book entitled *Ghosts*. Morwenstow surely is such a place to trigger ideas along those eerie lines. In his reign it must have been an even more remote place - had a more haunted air.

Though Hawker was at Morwenstow for more than four decades, he remained - to many local people – an enigma. He was undoubtedly a remarkable man, but, in the deepest sense, he was no better known to some than on the day he arrived. These, of course, were class-divided times, and many would have been in awe of a man who was both their parson and squire. Moreover there were contradictions in his make-up. At times he relished the solitutude of a medieval hermit, on other occasions, he enjoyed the social scene; outside and beyond that his was a self-sacrificing career in a very remote corner of the Church of England's Empire.

Nevertheless he achieved a great deal: a point Joan Rendell the Cornish Bard touched on in her earlier and now out of print Bossiney title *Cornish Churches*:

'Robert Stephen Hawker undoubtedly brought religion to Morwenstow. When he went there in 1834 he regarded it almost as a

HAWKER's cottage at Coombe. He must have been happy in this lovely secluded valley. Hawker and his wife lived here when he was studying for Holy Orders. An interesting legacy is the window he built in the shape of a cross. It consists of small panes of glass to let maximum light into his study. Hawker claimed the holy light encouraged and inspired him and, for all his life, the cross was a mystical symbol.

'country of savages' and indeed it was so remote and so wild in its grandeur of cliffs and sea that its inhabitants had for generations concentrated on survival rather than on the teachings of Christ or any other aspect of the church. Hawker changed all that. It was an uphill task but one to which he dedicated himself wholeheartedly and from viewing him with suspicion and even hate when he first arrived in the parish, his parishioners came to love and highly respect him.'

Unorthodox and unconventional, learned and impulsive, generous and indiscreet – he was all these and a great deal more. Like his grandfather, Dr Hawker of Charles Church, Plymouth, he was ready to give away almost everything he had. On wild winter nights he would have curious intuitions about those who might need some extra food or bed covering. Prompted by such inner feelings, he would gather together blankets, food and even wine and, accompanied by a servant, would set out and subsequently knock at the door of the cottage in question.

Physically, he was tall and well-built, his voice so rich and powerful that he could carry on a conversation with a neighbour at a farm on the other side of the valley.

In a sentence he was a man of remarkable, even strange, individuality: a character of impulse; yes, a law unto himself. His impulses were good, his heart full of kindness and his generosity knew no bounds.

HAWKER cut an impressive figure at church services. Robed in beautiful vestments, he administered rites with great dignity, but there was invariably the human element in his ministry. For example, during the Sacrament of Holy Baptism he had the habit of pinching the child to make it squeal 'to let the Devil out ...' At a wedding too he had a little ritual of tossing the ring into the air and catching it 'for luck for the happy couple'.

He could, though, be caustic. A dissenter came to him one day: someone who had just lost a relative. 'Bury a dissenter,' replied the Parson, 'I shall be delighted. I should like to bury the lot!'

Often he had services on weekdays, and when the moment came for the sexton to cease ringing, Hawker would shout down the church: 'Now, John, three for the Trinity and one for The Blessed Virgin!' Then the service would commence.

Sitting quietly in his church we can perhaps in the eye of our imagination see how it was in his day. That, in a curious way, is the measure of the impact he made – and makes.

31

ST NECTAN's Church at Welcombe, drawn by Felicity Young of Tintagel. Saint Nectan's fame spread far beyond Cornwall and Devon where there are five dedications to him. He was the eldest son of King Brychan of Brecknock's big family. When Robert Stephen Hawker was made curate here it must have been a desolate spot. Hawker never forgot his encounter with the Demon. Thereafter he sang hymns – and sang them loudly – whenever he rode through these valleys. The atmosphere of the region worked on his writer's imagination too, for it is generally considered he based his novel **Cruel Coppinger** *on this coastline.*

Did Cruel Coppinger belong to fact or fiction?
Joy Wilson, who contributed a chapter in **Westcountry Mysteries,** *introduced by her husband Colin – a now out of print Bossiney title – wrote: 'Was he just a satanic folk-hero? Is it safe to assume that "Cruel Coppinger" never existed? There are many documented facts which indicate that Coppinger really was in North Devon at that time. But the question is which Coppinger? Therein lies the mystery …'*
That perceptive travel writer Arthur Mee came here in the 1930s and wrote in his notebook 'Welcombe. It is as if it were saying to the traveller coming from Cornwall, Welcome into Devon, for this lonely little place is at the Cornish border.'

PARSON Hawker knew all about the importance of education, and St Mark's School at Shop is a lasting monument of that fact. By the year 1843 he had designed – in the shape of a cross – and built the school. He furnished it at personal expense and provided a residence for the schoolmaster. The sad truth is the school was a constant drain on his finances, but he would rejoice in the knowledge that St Mark's flourishes to this day. Our photograph shows pupils at the school celebrating 150 years.

The creation of this school is a further reminder of Hawker's ability as an all-rounder and his contribution in improving the quality of life in the district. Politically he was something of a radical but he was devoted to Crown and Constitution. We know that in 1857 he voted for Mr Robarts, later Lord Robarts, who was a Liberal but in 1873 he was enthusiastic for the return of a Conservative for Exeter. At heart he was champion of the labouring classes and when he spoke on the subject of social justice the words came with the eloquence and energy of a prophet.

HIS BALLADS

Hawker's robust ballads captured the remoteness of the Cornwall of his day, and in his verse he breathed life and vitality into legend and myth. His work was valued by literary characters like Charles Dickens and Sir Walter Scott, and Tennyson himself once admitted 'Hawker has beaten me on my own ground.' On the death of his first wife Charlotte, a combination of grief and opium fired him to write his tour de force *The Quest of Sangraal*. One critic described it as 'the most successful poem directly inspired by the Arthurian legend ...' Though Tintagel was more than twenty miles away, Hawker was very much under the Arthurian spell. He had honeymooned there with Charlotte and made repeated visits: 'If I could but throw myself back to King Arthur's time.'

But he gained his immortality with *The Song of the Western Men*:

And shall Trelawny die?
Then twenty thousand Cornishmen
Will know the reason why!

Hawker composed his immortal lines not in his hut on the cliffs but sitting in Sir Bevil Grenville's 'Walk' in lovely Stowe Wood. He posted it to the *Royal Devonport Telegraph & Plymouth Chronicle* who duly published it anonymously. Davies Gilbert of Tredea, President of the Royal Society, reading it and seeing its worth, sent it - as he thought- as his find of an old traditional ballad to the *Gentleman's Magazine*. Its fame was hastened by Macaulay quoting it in his History, and Dickens reprinting it in *Household Words*. But nearly four decades on Hawker wrote: *'All these years the Song has been bought and sold, set to music and applauded, while I have lived on among these far away rocks (Morwenstow) unprofited, unpraised and unknown . . .'*

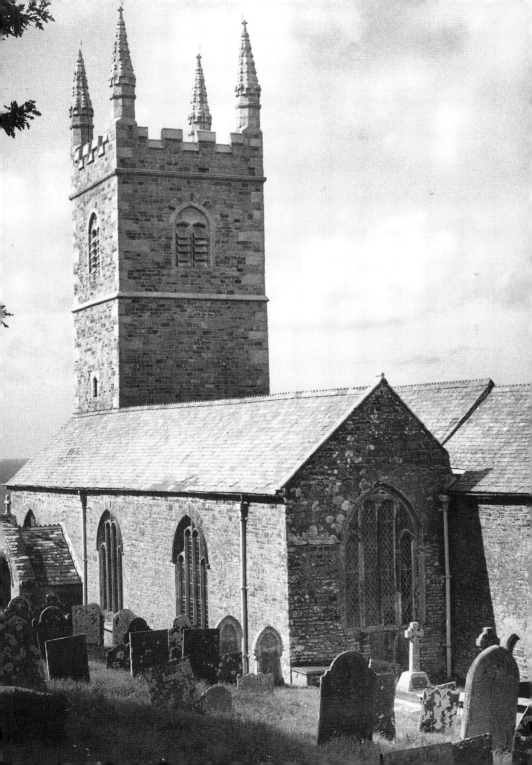

THE COAST

This is a wicked coastline and Robert Stephen Hawker probably summed it up in just two lines:

From Hartland Point to Padstow Light
Is a watery grave by day and by night.

These basic facts underline the cruel nature of these coastal waters. Between 1824 and 1874, the year in which the lighthouse on Hartland Point was built, there were more than eighty wrecks in this area. In 1832 a resident of Poughill, hard by Bude, wrote an account of some 37 wrecks between Morwenstow and St Gennys in less than a hundred years.

Here is Hawker describing gruesome events in a letter to a friend:

'Did I or did I not mention the wreck of the 'Ben Coolen' East Indiaman, at Bude, on the 21st October – crew thirty-two, six saved alive, twenty-six drowned?

'The channel is full of wreck – cargo – and among it corpses. Thirteen came ashore at Bude at the time of the wreck, some lashed to the raft: these are buried all in one pit in Bude Churchyard. This I do not call a Christian burial. We have lived in continual horror ever since, i.e. in sad and solemn expectation of the dead. Accordingly on Tuesday, the 4th, the message came at night. "A corpse ashore, sir, at Stanbury Mouth" – a creek a mile south. I order a strong coffin and the corpse is locked in for the night. I write a letter for the Coroner, and deliver it for transit to the police: and the the "misery" begins. Instead of a direct "messenger" the Parish Constable, by a new, and therefore clumsy loathsome law, the letter is passed on from parish to parish, through four or five hands, some at home, some to be searched for in the night; and thus, by this vague and tardy line of successional police, my letter only arrives with the Coroner at noon next day. He fills up, at my request, a warrant to bury, the inquest being uncalled for; but being sent by the same mode, I do not receive it until noon on Thursday, and by that time the poor dissolving carcass of Adam, seventeen days dead, has so filled the surrounding air, that it is only by a strong effort of my own, and by drenching my men with gin (for bearers) that I can fulfil that duty which must be done . . . and a few days since I was startled at night with a message – "a woman

Figurehead of the Caledonia Morwenstow photo Bode

THIS Edwardian picture postcard shows the 'Caledonia' figurehead above the path in the churchyard. In 1968 this treasured figurehead disappeared and was recovered by the police three weeks later in a field near Bideford. Local landlord Jim Gregory discounted the theory that local people had anything to do with it, explaining 'they wouldn't be seen within one hundred yards of it at night ... they regard it both with awe and dread.'

LOOKING towards the sea at Morwenstow.

has brought a man's right foot, sir, picked up at Combe". This we have laid in the ground, till perhaps its body too may come; and now with twelve bodies still unfound and the set of the current always urging on the creeks of Morwenstow, you will understand the nervous, wretched state in which we listen all day and all night for those thrilling knocks at the door, which announce the advent of the dead.'

On another occasion Hawker wrote: The Wreck of the *Margaret Quayle*, of Liverpool, 1,050 tons, of cargo salt, on Friday, December 4th 1863 – A cry at sunrise – a ship lying dismasted one mile off Hennacliff. Rushed out. Saw men on board the hull. Ship at anchor. In. Wrote a note to the coxwain of the Bude Lifeboat: "Put your boat on her wheels, get horses at my expense, and hasten up towards us – putting to sea at the first feasible creek, to take off the crew." Out again on my cliff with a glass. Saw the crew in knots on board, to and from: presently a boat lowered. Five men got in, pointing for Marsland Mouth. Got my pony and Mr Valentine his. Rode up to Hennacliff and then on along the cliff brink, side by side, as the boat rowed. Up and down hill and valley. Boat heading. Still upward, sometimes under the waves, then mounting them; on to Speke's Mill, on to Hartland Quay, allowed no signal to be made.

Surf near shore too high for boat to live. At last watched her round the point and saw them make Clovelly Bay safe. Down to Hartland Quay, saw coastguard, got them to promise to watch all night, turned towards our own cliffs again. Dusk. Saw when we got near Marsland again another boat lowered; saw her staved on the ship's side, washed ashore at the mill, four oars, no men.'

Nothing symbolizes Hawker's ministry at Morwenstow more poignantly than the strange white monument, on the left above the narrow path which slopes down the churchyard to the main door. It is the figurehead of the *Caledonia*, a two-hundred-ton sailing ship from Arbroath which ran aground nearby in a terrible gale in 1842. There was only one survivor. All the other men aboard died and Hawker, to his considerable credit, located every body and buried them here.

HAWKER'S HUT

Hawker's hut on the cliffs must be the smallest property owned by the National Trust. He built the original little building from driftwood which he hauled up from the beach below. Here you feel very close to the spirit of the man, the seclusion appealing to the mystic in him. Here he wrote his poems and books, his songs and some of his sermons - and answered much of his mail.

Hawker looked forward to his letters with the keen anticipation of a child at Christmas. When the postman passed by, without calling, he was bitterly disappointed. Each day was usually carefully mapped out, and on fine evenings he and his wife would wait for the postman who normally came around tea-time. They would then walk out to the hut, read his letters and answer them there on the spot. In his early days at Morwenstow he had to collect his letters from Shop, some two miles away, and he paid a girl two pence a week to fetch his mail.

Here too in his hut he sat and quietly smoked his pipes of opium and meditated. From this spot he also shaped his own weather forecasts, brooding on the possibilities of storm and shipwreck.

This tiny building is an important destination on any tour of Hawker Country. Inside it you feel attuned to something deeper, more profound than a place of interest and curiosity. For some it may be the self-discovery of solitude. Hawker must have found it a great release - and some of that quality remains today. In fact, the modern pilgrim may come away refreshed and renewed.

The region of his hut provides a magnificent grandstand view of the coastline and the sea, and though he could be a social man Baring-Gould believed 'His best companions were the waves and clouds.' Despite his vitality and versatility, he lived 'the ever alone,' as he called himself in one of his letters, solitary 'in the Morwenstow ark with only the sound of the waters about him.'

He was in fact, a very fine letter writer and in one piece of correspondence recalled the wreckers' old toast:

'A billowy sea and a shattering wind,
The cliffs before, and the gale behind.'

But concluded '… thank God, no wrecks yet on our iron shore.'

This is an awe-inspiring spot on a wild day when the spindrift comes bounding up the cliffs. Sitting here, where he sat, you will discover

Hawker, after all, is not far away and that Cornwall is different things to different people. Moreover what she has to offer must be received individually and with humility.

The settings in which authors write tell us a good deal about them. Lawrence of Arabia found his inspiration and release in a secluded cottage in Dorset. Samuel Taylor Coleridge wrote his most enduring works in a lonely farmhouse at Nether Stowey, Somerset. Hawker, for his part, did his writing here or in his lovely vicarage and, unlike the majority of vicars of his day, he wrote on a wide range of subjects and apart from his professional authorship he was a busy letter writer. We can safely assume that much of his poetry was written here in the hut inspired by this often tempestuous North Cornwall - North Devon coast.

HIS WIVES
AND HIS END

Chapters of Hawker's life read like pages of fiction from a novel written by an imaginative novelist. His two marriages underline that fact. His wives could not have been more different. He was an undergraduate at Oxford University when he married his first wife, Charlotte, a daughter of Colonel Wrey I'ans of Whitstone who was his godmother – then aged 41! In his University days, married, it was arranged his wife's two sisters should come to live with them and he became known as 'the man with three wives.'

The influence of Charlotte was considerable. A woman of poetic, refined mind, she helped him through times of depression giving him sound guidance when impetuosity robbed him of balanced judgement. She was his wife for nearly forty years and her passing wounded him deeply.

However he found happiness in a second marriage. It says much for his attractive personality that he was able to woo and wed an intelligent and high spirited girl forty years his junior. Pauline Kuczynski, the daughter of an English lady married to an exiled Pole, was employed as a governess to a Yorkshire vicar's children. They came to Morwenstow when the Reverend W Valentine needed to convalesce in the sea air of North Cornwall.

Hawker fell deeply in love with the younger woman who bore him three daughters. The feelings were mutual, but it is said he was saddened by the fact that she failed to produce a son.

In the last years, Hawker's health declined seriously; the prospects of his family oppressed him, anxieties gnawed. In June, 1875, he stayed

PAULINE, the second Mrs Hawker. The parson adored his young second wife, the daughter of an English lady married to an exiled Pole. She came to Morwenstow as the governess to a Yorkshire vicar's children, when the Reverend W Valentine needed to convalesce in the sea air of North Cornwall. Hawker wrote of her '... a young woman with a Face and Form to win an Emperor.' Nevertheless she remained a central tantalising figure in the controversy surrounding his deathbed conversion to the Roman Catholic Church.

with his brother at Boscastle, who, in a letter, described him as 'very ill, and certainly broken in his mind.' By the end of August, Robert Stephen Hawker was in his coffin in Plymouth Cemetery – a Roman Catholic. His end is cloaked in confusion and controversy.

Pauline Hawker had taken him to Plymouth for medical advice. There he had suffered a paralytic stroke, and on the Saturday before his death, Mrs Hawker sent for the Roman Catholic, Canon Mansfield. She later insisted that such an invitation was at the request of her husband. Sabine Baring-Gould, though, in his biography *The Vicar of Morwenstow* clearly stated: *'Through the kindness of Mr Hawker's relatives I have been furnished with every letter that passed on the subject of his death, and reception into Roman communion. In not one of them is it asserted that he asked to have Canon Mansfield sent for: the last expression of a wish was that he might go back to Morwenstow.'*

Baring-Gould's biography, it is fair to say, does contain some inaccuracies. But that wish to 'go back to Morwenstow' has an authentic ring. Hawker, after all, had given 41 years of his life to the parish. Nevertheless Pauline Hawker should have known her husband's innermost thoughts. Or did she? Her belief was that he had been 'at heart a Roman Catholic' for some years.

Baring-Gould's biography *The Vicar of Morwenstow* was first published in 1876, only one year after Hawker's death, and this might be the place to quote a few lines from the last chapter:

'I think it possible, that during the last year or two of his life, when failing mentally as well as bodily and when labouring under the excitement or subsequent depression caused by the opium he ate to banish pain, he may have said, or written recklessly, words which are capable of being twisted into meaning a change of views. There can be little doubt that the taking of narcotics deadens the moral sense, the appreciation of Truth, and possibly, towards the end, Mr Hawker may have had hankerings Romeward. But we must consider the man as he was when sound in body and in mind, and not when stupefied by pain, and the medicines given to deaden the pain.'

Was Hawker capable of making a decision to join the Roman Catholic Church at this sick, late stage in his life? Or did he hang on at Morwenstow because he loved the place so? Or did he stay for purely material reasons? Or did he profess Roman Catholicism privately and yet publicly perform as an Anglican parson?

These are only some of the questions in what was a religious row and remains a riddle. We shall probably never now get to the bottom of it. This much is certain: in the hearts of many Cornish people, Hawker will - for ever - be the Vicar of Morwenstow.

DRAWING of Robert Stephen Hawker by Felicity Young, based on a sketch by the Earl of Carlisle in 1863.

HAWKER'S school.

TWO lanes meeting at Shop.

About the Author

A Cornishman, Michael Williams has been publishing for more than twenty years. He and his wife Sonia live in a cottage on the shoulder of a green valley outside St Teath in North Cornwall. Outside his Bossiney activities, he is a writing and publishing consultant, evaluating manuscripts and advising writers on their publishing prospects.

He has a special interest in Parson Hawker and Morwenstow having featured in a six episode series on the subject for BBC Radio Cornwall. A regular visitor to Morwenstow, Michael Williams has been researching and writing about Hawker and his parish for more than twenty years. 'I feel I have come to know Robert Stephen Hawker reasonably well,' he says, 'but he remains an enigma in many ways – sometimes a very puzzling figure in life and death. Though, of course, Morwenstow itself remains one of our Cornish gems.'

Acknowledgements

I am indebted to Jill Savage of Rectory Farm for her encouragement in putting together *About Hawker & Morwenstow*. Thanks also to those who have given interviews or allowed me to quote from their published work and to the Local Studies Library at Redruth in particular. Once more I owe much to the visual contributions of Felicity Young and Ray Bishop, cover design by Maggie Ginger, editing by Angela Larcombe and the manuscript work of Sally Dodd. This then is a team effort and, within the context of Bossiney publishing, a fresh look at Hawker and his Kingdom.

MORE BOSSINEY BOOKS ...

EDGE OF THE UNKNOWN
Michael Williams
'These investigations into psychic phenomena are some of the more fascinating in more than thirty years of ghost hunting.'

PSYCHIC PHENOMENA of the WEST
Michael Williams
The subject of a Daphne Skinnard interview on BBC Radio Cornwall.
'Michael Williams continues his well-known researches into the strange and the inexplicable ... cases range from cornwall to Wiltshire ...'
The Cornish Guardian

SUPERSTITION AND FOLKLORE
Michael Williams
A survey of Westcountry Superstitions: Interviews on the subject and some Cornish and Devon folklore.
'... the strictures that we all ignore at our peril. To help us keep out of trouble, Mr Williams has prepared a comprehensive list.'
Frank Kempe, North Devon Journal-Herald

SECRET CORNWALL
Introduced by Madeleine Gould of BBC Radio Cornwall

THE CORNISH WORLD OF DAPHNE du MAURIER
Contains a previously unpublished chapter by Dame Daphne

DISCOVERING BODMIN MOOR
E.V. Thompson

KING ARTHUR IN THE WEST
Felicity Young & Michael Williams

We shall be pleased to send you our catalogue giving full details of our growing list of titles and forthcoming publications. If you have difficulty in obtaining our titles, write direct to Bossiney Books, Land's End, St Teath, Bodmin, Cornwall.